Max Martin

Analysis of Greenhouse Gas Emissions for Flower Producers in Ecuador

Anchor Academic
Publishing

Martin, Max: Analysis of Greenhouse Gas Emissions for Flower Producers in Ecuador, Hamburg, Anchor Academic Publishing 2016

Buch-ISBN: 978-3-95489-387-4
PDF-eBook-ISBN: 978-3-95489-885-5
Druck/Herstellung: Anchor Academic Publishing, Hamburg, 2016

Bibliografische Information der Deutschen Nationalbibliothek:
Die Deutsche Nationalbibliothek verzeichnet diese Publikation in der Deutschen Nationalbibliografie; detaillierte bibliografische Daten sind im Internet über http://dnb.d-nb.de abrufbar.

Bibliographical Information of the German National Library:
The German National Library lists this publication in the German National Bibliography. Detailed bibliographic data can be found at: http://dnb.d-nb.de

© Anchor Academic Publishing, Imprint der Diplomica Verlag GmbH
Hermannstal 119k, 22119 Hamburg
http://www.diplomica-verlag.de, Hamburg 2016
Printed in Germany

Executive Summary

The goal of this study is the calculation of greenhouse gas emissions which occur during the production of Ecuadorian Flowers. Emissions are considered beginning with the production of raw materials up to the point where the flowers are sold to the final wholesale.

In the beginning the current status of international standardisation is described with their relevance to the calculation. Currently there are no official regulations for CO2 calculations. Because most of the flowers are sold to Europe the Life Cycle Assessment (LCA) regulations ISO 14040 ff have been applied for the methodology and the creation of the system model. The importance of this standard has been pointed out as it will be the basis for upcoming European CO2 regulations. Nowadays a widely accepted method is the greenhouse gas protocol which has been used partly for the calculations because only few sectors (e.g. transportation) are covered.

Chapter 2 introduces the model of flower production. The model includes all processes and the system boundaries. Significant factors contributing to the greenhouse gas emissions are defined as airfreight of flower to the final market, consumption of electricity and usage of fertilizers on the farm.

The process of collecting data is subject of Chapter 3 including the last audit data from the Flower Label Program (FLP) as well as independently created inquiries and visits on the pilot farms.

Chapter 4 comprises the calculation of CO2 emissions. The sources of the emissions factors are described in the beginning, which are mostly extracted from LCA software. The results illustrated in Figure 1 prove the assumptions of the main contribution factors.

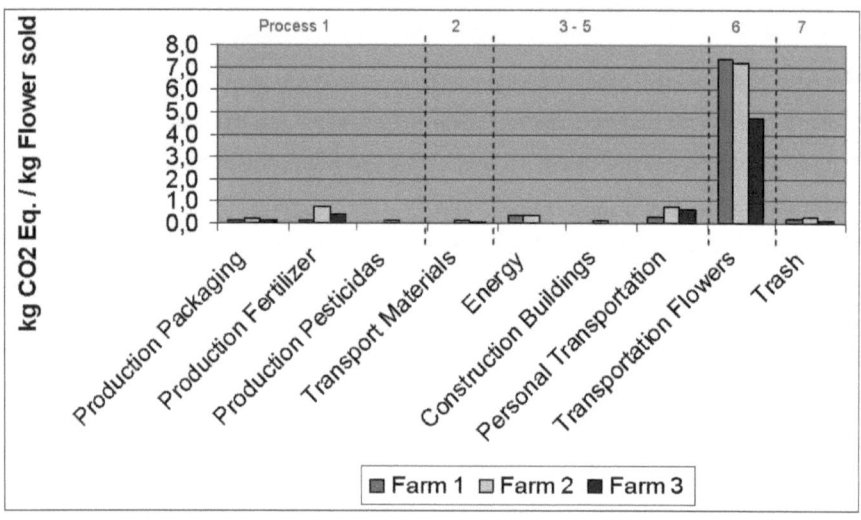

Figure 1: Overview of CO2 Emissions for Flowers

The calculation results in flower emissions varying from 6 to 10 kg CO2 equivalents for 1 kg flower sold.

Chapter 5 proposes the next steps on the way to CO2 neutral flowers. Firstly the calculation has to be certified by an independent organisation. Subsequently a decision on CO2 compensation has to be taken. The purchase of CO2 certificates from official or voluntary stock exchanges was recommended because self managed CO2 projects need start-up time. The last step is the marketing of the new product, which should be realized with a CO2 label widely accepted in the distribution markets. Parallel the farms should start to optimize their farms according to CO2 emissions. Recommendations can be found in Chapter 6.

Since global warming potential is only one measurement of interference with nature other criteria should be investigated as: How is the quality of ground water? To what extend occurs acidification in the cultivated areas? An integrated LCA analysis would give answers to these questions.

Table of Contents

Abbreviations

BSI	British Standard Institute
C	Carbon
CO_2	Carbon Dioxide
CORDELIM	Oficina Nacional de Promoción del MDL de Ecuador
EnEV	Energieeinsparverordnung (German energy regulation for buildings)
EU	European Union
DEFRA	Department for Environmental Food and rural Affairs
FLP	Flower Label Program
GaBi	Ganzheitliche Bilanzierung, LCA Software by the University of Stuttgart
GDP	Gross Domestic Product
GEMIS	Globales Emissions-Modell Integrierter Systeme
GHG	Greenhouse Gas
GTAP	Global Trade Analysis Project
IPCCC	Intergovernmental Panel on Climate Change
ISO	International Organisation for Standardisation
K	Potassium
LCA	Life Cycle Assessment
LCI	Life Cycle Inventory
N	Nitrogen
NGO	Non Government Organisation
P	Phosphor
PAS	Publicly Available Specification
UNEP	United Nations Environmental Program
UNFCCC	United Nations Framework Convention on Climate Change
WBCSD	World Business Council for Sustainable Development
WRI	World Research Institute

Table of Figures

Table of Tables

Introduction

In 2007 the Intergovernmental Panel on Climate Change (IPCC) illustrated the urgency of actions to mitigate global warming in their fourth assessment report.[1] Figure 2 is extracted from the report and shows clearly how global temperature increases with higher concentration of Greenhouse Gases (GHG). The increase in temperature is a global average. Since microclimates also have a strong influence on local climate different effects will take place to local climates.

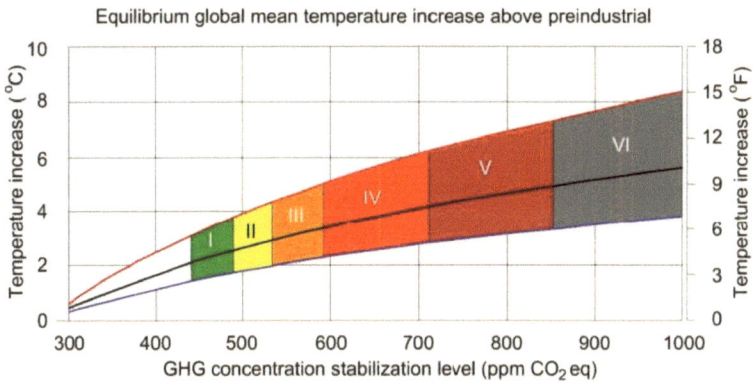

Figure 2: Correlation between GHG Concentration and Temperature Increase[2]

Currently the agricultural sector is responsible for at least 12,5 % of the GHG emissions worldwide. Further 10% are due to changes in land use which are often caused by turning grassland into agricultural production. [3]

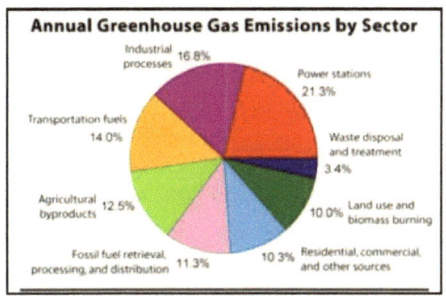

Figure 3: GHG Emissions by Sector[4]

[1] IP07WG4
[2] WI08GR
[3] IP07WG3, also see Figure 3: GHG Emissions by Sector

Though the majority of these emissions are based on livestock breeding, the flower industry as part of this sector uses lots of resources for growing and selling flowers. For example transportation by air freight to markets in Russia, Europe and the US causes lots of CO2 emissions.

At the same time agricultural organisations are strongly affected by the consequences of global warming in terms of weather and temperature uncertainties. [5] This causes agricultural organisation to take action regarding to reducing CO2 emissions. Additionally political subsidies for efficient CO2 reduction methods must be introduced. The beginning of all is a CO2 analysis which is subject to this study.

Goal

The demand of CO2 neutral products has increased recently. 55% of the German population is willing to pay higher prices if the products are CO2 neutral.[6] Dole as the world biggest fruit producer and distributor entered the market of CO2 neutrality.[7] The FLP organisation certifies flower production with the FLP label. This guarantees the client that the product was produced according to the FLP standards which include social and ecological standards.[8] FLP also wants to offer clients CO2 neutral flowers to strengthen the distribution channel for their members. Therefore the goal of the study is the calculation of CO2 emissions calculated per flower sold.

Since the customer is the point of reference emissions that are emitted during the entire lifecycle of a flower have to be considered and calculated.

Approach

Firstly it was investigated if international standards are available and could be used for calculating CO2 emissions. (Chapter 1) Secondly a model for flower production was designed with all the processes and production applied (Chapter 2). This was the basis for the data collection consisting of inquiries and personal visits (Chapter 3). In Chapter 4 the calculation is described with each emissions factor used. Finally a recommendation for the next steps is given (Chapter 5) and further scientific tasks which came up during this study presented in Chapter 6.

---

[4] WI08GR
[5] SC08ROL
[6] HUB08CMP
[7] HA07DO
[8] FL07GU

1 Standards and Methodology

CO2 calculations often cannot be retraced because transparency of the calculations steps and standardized factors for emissions are missing. The internet offers many CO2 calculators for certain areas (e.g. personal transportation). In the majority of the cases it is not clearly stated what system is being analyzed, what methodology is being applied and where the system boundaries are.

On the other hand companies offer CO2 compensation for CO2 emissions. Analogical the methodologies and boundaries for those compensations are different and hard to compare. In the following the main standards and software solutions are described.

1.1 *Standards for Calculating CO2 Emissions*

This chapter includes various different methodologies which have evolved to calculate CO2 emissions. These vary as the ISO standards only offer methodological standards and other norms also offer calculation data.

1.1.1 National Greenhouse Gas Inventories Programme

The IPCC was established in 1998 by the United Nations Environment Programme (UNEP) and the World Meteorological Organization (WMO). The organisation publishes reports on climate change and evaluates the risk of climate change provoked by human activity.

Already before that, in 1991, the IPCC National Greenhouse Gas Inventories Programme was created with two main goals. Firstly to develop an internationally accepted method and software for the calculation of national greenhouse gases. Secondly to publish and spread the methodology to all the members of the United Nations Framework Convention on Climate Change (UNFCCC[9]).

---

[9] The UNFCCC currently consists of 189 member states who meet at a yearly climate conference.

1.1.2 ISO 14040

The ISO 14040 standard consists of a Life Cycle Assessment Framework which includes four different stages. The standard is applied for various reasons. Companies try to reduce costs by making production more efficient. Therefore an LCA can be used to compare different ways of production in order to enhance production by using less resources or reducing emissions.

Another application is the strategic planning of investments or products. The NGO for example proposes a new product called "CO2 neutral flowers". Therefore the emissions have to be calculated in detail. The ISO 14040 method would assure the client that the calculations are based on standardized procedure.

By calculating LCA public policy makers get the awareness of the relative consumption of resources and emissions in the different stages of production. Thus, specific regulations can be processed. Finally Marketing uses the results for economical growth.

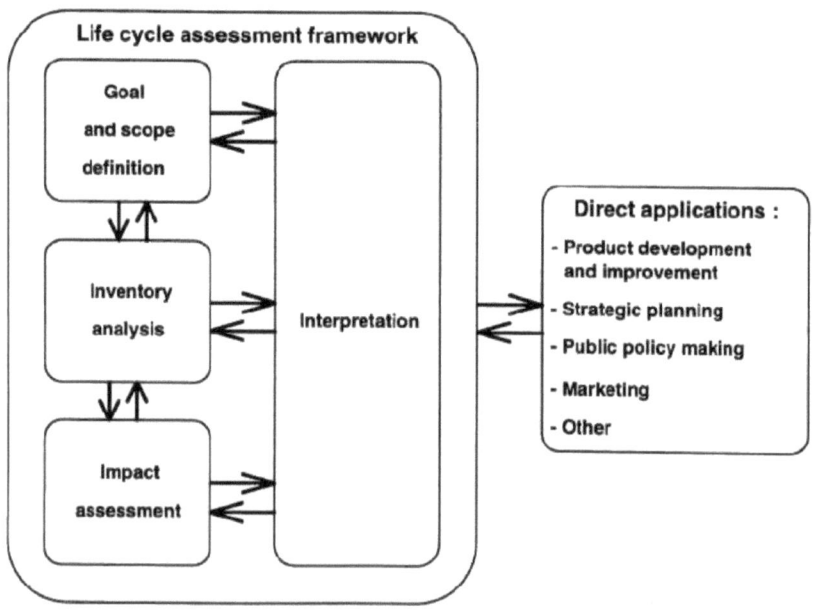

Figure 4: Life Cycle Assessment Framework[10]

---

[10] ISO07

The four stages in Figure 4 have to be passed to provide compliance to the ISO norm. Each stage influences each other. Therefore the analysis is adopted with small adoptions:

1. Goal and scope

   The first phase consists of a description and specification of the goal and the scope of the calculation. This leads to a definition of the system boundaries. The system boundaries determine if emissions are included in the calculation. Separately the object that is being investigated has to be described in detail. It is also referred to as *functional unit*.

2. Life Cycle Inventory (LCI)

   The second phase includes the creation of the data inventory. This can be carried out by using dedicated LCA software, also referred to as "one source approach", or by connecting various sources of information such as expert data or literature. The data has to be described and verified. All data has to be related to the functional unit which is defined in the goal and scope definition.

   In the following a consistent model is created which included all relevant unit processes within the system boundaries. Each process consists of specific inputs and outputs. Examples for inputs are raw materials, chemicals fuels or electricity. Outputs are air and water emissions or solid waste.

   The result is a life cycle inventory. This includes detailed unit processes with all inputs and outputs in the form of elementary flows from and to the environment. According to ISO 14044 an elementary flow is defined as:

   "*a) material or energy entering the system being studied, which has been drawn from the environment without previous human transformation, or; b) material or energy leaving the system being studied, which is discarded into the environment without subsequent human transformation*"[11]

   At this stage interpretation is acceptable. The standard accepts different interpretation in different unit processes if those are „fair" and justified.

---

[11] IS06EN

3. Life Cycle Impact Assessment

Each elementary flow has to be allocated to environmental impact categories such as global warming, eutrophication) or acidification. This first step is called characterization. The impact potentials are calculated based on the results of the life cycle inventory.

The next step is the weighting by assigning the impact categories a weighting factor depending on their relative importance. According to ISO standard this is voluntary as the next step normalization.

Since the different impact categories have different units, normalization aims at one calculable unit.

4. Interpretation

The last stage is the most important one. It contains analysis of major contributions, sensitivity analysis and uncertainty analysis. The interpretation of these determines if the ambitions set in the first phase can be met. Conclusions are extracted from this phase, which should be reviewed critically before being published.

1.1.3 GHG Indicator

The United Nations Environmental Program (UNEP) issued a report in 2000 on how to calculate GHG emissions. The procedure is transformed into spreadsheets managed by the World Research Institute (WRI) and the World Business Council for Sustainable Development (WBCSD). These spreadsheets are described more in detail in Chapter 4.1.3.

"*The guidelines provide a methodology whereby GHG emissions are calculated, then combined to give a single-figure GHG Indicator for an organisation's contribution to climate change.*"[12]

The procedure however includes the definition of system boundaries. Subsequently the usage of fuels, electricity, cooling/heating plantations, product/personal transportation and process emissions are collected. Conversion factors are provided by the method to receive CO2 equivalent based results.

---

[12] THOOTH, page 10

The final results are normalized by using categories and connecting the results to the single units of the category. For example one category is production and all the emissions that are in this category such as electricity, process emissions and product transportation are summed up and divided by the quantity of products which are produced. This gives an indicator of CO_2 equivalents per product.

Carbon offsets such as reforested areas are not considered in this method. Data on process related GHG emissions is not available in an extensive manner.

1.1.4 PAS 2050

The department for environmental food and rural affairs (DEFRA) and the Carbon Trust requested the British Standard Institute (BSI) to develop a Publicly Available Specification (PAS). The project aims to connect all current and relevant GHG calculation methods to form a single method of calculating embodied greenhouse gas emissions from goods and services. "*The PAS aims to bridge the gap between the existing detailed and more general approaches and provide a standardised, consistent method organisations can practically use for measuring the GHG emissions embodied in products and services.*"[13]

In February 2008 the last report "*Methods review to support the PAS for the calculation of the embodied greenhouse gas emissions of goods and services PAS 2050*" was published. The report recommends ISO-consistent hybrid LCA approach which combines process LCA with input and output analysis. Each sub-process is analysed and the CO_2 emissions calculated. These emissions are added through the process chain of a product. Parallel a financial balance is created which connects the prices of the product at the different stages with the emissions. If emissions from a sub-process cannot be calculated, the results of the financial balance are used. Since the retrieval of relevant data is more difficult compared to the methods, the PAS recommends using standardized data from the Global Trade Analysis Project (GTAP). It will take until 2010 until the British Office for National Statistics will publish environmental data that must be used for the calculation.

This approach is currently the most developed one in Europe but yet not finalized. Therefore, it is summarized but not applied in this study.

---

[13] BS08RE

1.2   *LCA software*

There are already software tools available, which can deal with hybrid LCA systems recommended by the PAS 2050 such as SimaPro, Bottomline or CMLCA. In 2000 the Swedish Environmental Research Institute summarized various LCA software in one report.[14]

The software data used for this study included *GEMIS* (Globales Emissions-Modell Integrierter Systeme), the free of charge LCA software of the institute of applied ecology, Freiburg (Ökoinstitut) and *GABI* (Ganzheitliche Bilanzierung) which is developed by the University of Stuttgart in cooperation with PE International. Also the Swiss based *econinvent* database which is managed by the Swiss Centre for Life Cycle Inventories including various research organisations.

1.3   *Applied Methodology*

The market of CO2 calculations is currently not very regulated and lacks one common standard. In the sector of LCA the new ISO 14040 was published in 2006 with a standardized methodology. This standard can be seen as the methodological basis for the CO2 standards and thus also for this study.

Other regulations as the PAS 2050 build on this regulation. Since the PAS is designated for the European Market which is the leading export market for Ecuadorian flowers this calculation standard should be applied when the final version is published.

The National Greenhouse Gas Inventories Programme and the GHG Indicator offer various calculation methods which are very useful for the calculation of this study.

In the designing phase of the project two different methodologies have been discussed with the project sponsor. Firstly a LCA analysis based on LCA software and secondly a CO2 analysis based on the methodologies of the LCA norms with different sources of data.

---

[14] JÖooLC

The first method is coupled to LCA software which was opposed by the project partner for several reasons. Therefore the procedure was adopted with the following work procedure:

1. **Analysis of the case to identify significant issues.**

   The case material is browsed and analyzed with focus on the final target audience and the purpose of the study.

2. **Definition of the scope for the case.**

   This step includes documentation of the system including the system boundaries.

3. **Data Inventory.**

   The need of data and documentation is identified. The data is collected, validated and documented.

4. **Preparation and calculation of the inventory profile in the case.**

   Data is related to the functional unit. System boundaries can be refined.

5. **Interpretation.**

   Interpret the results with the focus defined in the goal and scope.[15]

---

[15] adopted from LCA training package, page 3

2 Definition of the Flower Calculation Model

According to the methodology of DIN 14040 ff the beginning of the analysis contains the definition of the significant GHG contributors which will be described in this chapter amongst the goal of the study and the scope.

2.1 *Significant GHG Contribution Factors*

The US, Europe and Russia are the main markets for Ecuadorian flowers. The flowers have to be sold quickly before they fade. **Air transportation** is the solution to solve this conflict but it causes high emissions.

It is recognized that consumption of goods and services, also called indirect emissions, are highly responsible for the rise to GHG emissions. The calculation of these "embodied" emissions contributes to the total emissions of flower production. Therefore the **consumption of chemicals** in form of fertilizers and pesticides were assumed to be one of the significant factors.

Approximately 50% of the worldwide emissions are caused by the generation of electricity. On the farms **electricity** is used for the office buildings and at some farms also for cooling the flowers before they are transported to the airport.

In a comparable LCA the main factors also were transportation, usage of chemicals and electricity.[16]

2.2 *Description of the Flower Calculation Model*

Flower production was divided into 8 different processes. Each process has GHG emissions. Material streams have been used to calculate the means of production used at the various stages and their respective emissions.

Since it is intended to show reduction potential, the emissions from the means of production are calculated in the process where they can be reduced by the farm. For example if they apply fewer chemicals on the farm, fewer emissions occur because of less emissions during the production of chemicals. The consequence is lower CO2 emissions. The process model can be obtained from Figure 5: Defined Flower Production Model.

---

[16] JUN99CA, page 34f

The first process consists of the production of all means of production. The finished products such as chemicals and office products are transported to the flower farm. In the farm the means of production are used to grow flowers which are also flows from this point on.

The fourth process deals with the packaging of the flowers. For protection they are separated with little paper boxes to avoid damage to the blossom. The flowers are surrounded by plastic film and packed into a carton box, called *tobacco*. One tobacco consists of up to 150 flowers. For distribution purposes two *tobaccos* are grouped together. The result is one cage, which is the unit used for exportation.

One farm uses cooled trucks to bring the flowers to the national airport. This helps to extend the life of the cut flowers. The flowers are transported to the final destination by airplane or very rarely by boat.

The system also includes the combustion of transport material at the end of the lifecycle. Roses are being treated as GHG neutral as they emit the absorbed GHG when they are burned or decomposed.

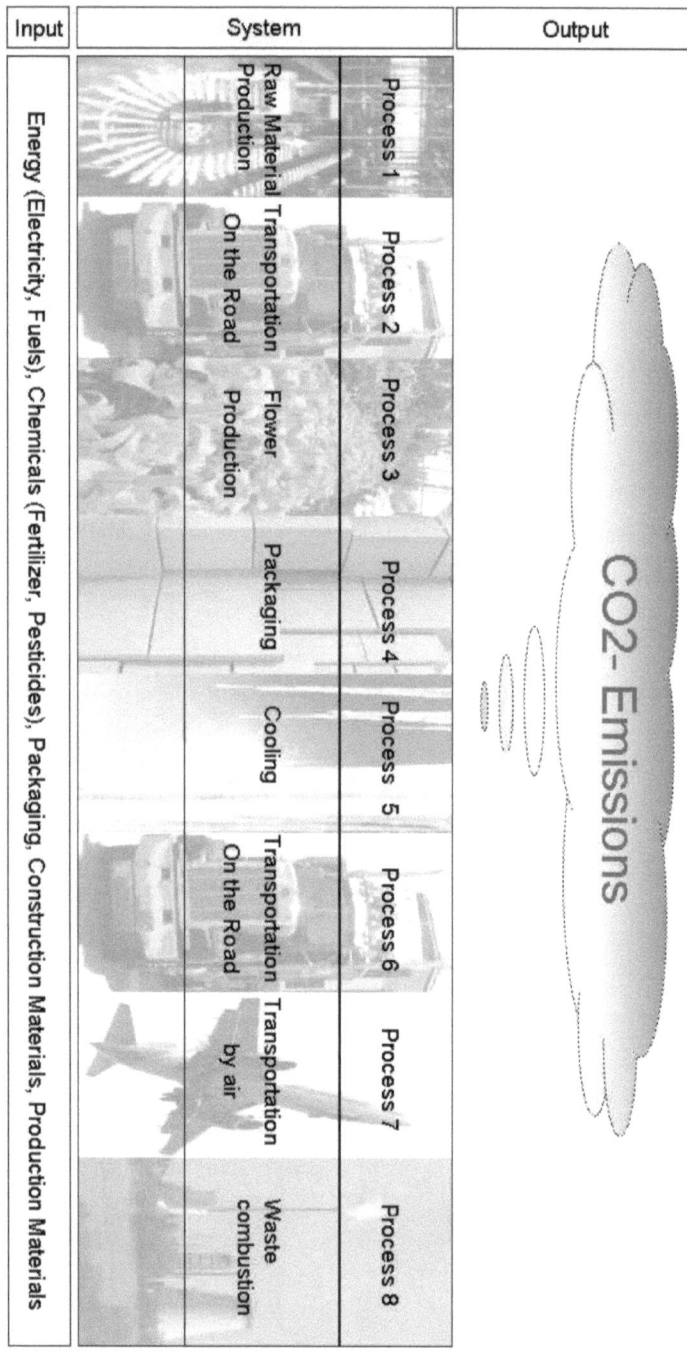

Input	System		Output
	Process 1	Raw Material Production	
	Process 2	Transportation On the Road	
	Process 3	Flower Production	
	Process 4	Packaging	CO2- Emissions
	Process 5	Cooling	
	Process 6	Transportation On the Road	
	Process 7	Transportation by air	
	Process 8	Waste combustion	
Energy (Electricity, Fuels), Chemicals (Fertilizer, Pesticides), Packaging, Construction Materials, Production Materials			

Figure 5: Defined Flower Production Model[17]

[17] Illustration by author

2.3   *General Assumptions and Exclusions*

Assumptions

According to the IPCC bedded GHG cannot be considered as a carbon sink because at the end of the lifecycle the GHG will be released to the nature. Around 30% of the volatile solids remain sequestered in the compost and released slowly over time.[18]

Exclusions

In contrast to the LCA no financial reflection of flower production has been made. Furthermore these subjects have been excluded from the study:

Subject	Reason
Means of Production	Low emissions for textile and protection materials against chemicals.
Vehicles	Contracted vehicles are used sometimes and emissions for vehicle production are comparably low calculated by the years of usage.
Soil and Water	No data was available for the utilization of chemicals on the soil and residues of ingredients in the water. Most of the water is also reused for the flower production.
Miniplants	Most flower farms buy the small plants at brewer. This part was excluded because the energy intensity is not very high as most of them are close to the farms and the main contributor transportation therefore is very low.

---

[18] DE04REW, page 42

Doubled emissions for air transportation	Different scientists found out, that emissions from aviation could be twice as high as currently calculated. The reason lays in the contribution of aviation induced cirrus clouds. "As in the IPCC report[19] the new TRADEOFF estimate does not include the contribution from aviation induced cirrus clouds. It is possible that the total aviation RF [radiative forcings] could be twice as large as the total RF given here."[20] Because further investigations yet have not finally proven the results of the study, the "normal" CO2 emissions on flight transportation have been applied.
Application of Pesticides	Emissions during the application of pesticides could not be determined. Emissions of the production of pesticides are part of the calculation.

Table 1: Exclusions from the study

---

[19] PRA99PO, page 185-215
[20] SAU00AV, page 6

3 Data Inventory

After the main contributors have been determined and the system borders defined the data collection is the next step. It was decided to use a two step method to ensure completeness and correctness of the data.

Firstly a data enquiry was created which included question to all consumptions and production data. The PAS refers to this data as primary data. Although it takes a lot of effort to receive all primary data, this ambition was made to calculate the emissions as realistic as possible.[21] This enquiry has been send to the pilot farms. It consisted of nine parts which are related to the elementary flows or the 8 processes described in Chapter 3.

The first part[22]contained general data of the farms such as direction, size of the farm or employees. The farm size varied between 15 and 47 hectare and the employment between 200 and 600 workers.

The production of the farms was subject of the second part, the third part dealt with the elementary flow of fuels used.

Transportation was subject to the fourth part and included the transportation of employees, means of production to the farm, business trips of employees and the transport of flowers to the final vendor, mostly to the US, Europe and Russia.

Consumption of water, external electricity and internal generation was asked for in part 5.

The usage of chemicals was matter of the next part including country of production and content of the main ingredients nitrogen (N), phosphor (P) and potassium (K) for fertilizers and percentage of active ingredient for pesticides.

In part 7 the packaging and other means of production such as protective clothing and printing paper were covered.

Finally the farms had the chance to include missed emissions in part 9.

Each requested number (consumption, production data, etc.) received a unique identity in the enquiry. The number was put in the calculation later to retrace the source data.

The backflow of the farms was different. While most farms returned complete data, one farm returned only little information. After the reception of the filled enquiries

---

[21] A comparable study of the organisation myclimate used secondary data. It was intended to compare the data, but the myclimate study contained a lot of private data.
[22] See the appendix for the enquiry developed

every farm was visited to collect the missing data and to discuss contradictory data of the mass flows. The calculation of the mass balance helps to avoid mistakes.[23] The input of production goods is compared to the output of finished materials and waste. Data is missing if one value is higher than the other.

Additionally data from the audits of FLP were used to verify the data quality. FLP recertifies every farm each year and collects general data such as utilization of pesticides, fertilizers and electricity. This information helped to identify deviated data.

4 Calculation and Results

In this chapter all emissions are processed in the same manner. Realistic factors for each elementary flow are described with data sources and the cumulated emissions illustrated in figures. The emphasis was put on the main contributing factors. Low utilization of a mean of production resulted in less effort of finding an appropriate factor.

To compare the data of the different farms normalization is applied as recommended by ISO. The emissions of farms are normalized to kilogram CO2 equivalents per kilogram rose exported.

The first unit [kg CO2 Eq.] is used because CO2 is the "leading" greenhouse gas. Therefore emissions are calculated as CO2 equivalents. Because GHG's have a different exposure time the period considered is defined with 100 years.

The second unit [per kg rose] is chosen because the flowers of the different farms have a different weight which differs from 14 – 64 grams for summer flowers and 63 – 88 grams for roses.

---

[23] JUN99CA, page 48

4.1 Data Sources for the Emissions Factors

In the last publication of the PAS it was stated that "*it is [not] sufficient to simply record the source of secondary used. We agree with the majority of experts that a selected number of secondary data sources should be endorsed by the PAS.*"[24] Since the sources are currently not endorsed by the PAS and the intention is to correlate the standard to ISO, ISO based software and data was preferred. The applied sources are described in the following chapters. An overview of all sources used to calculate the emission factors can be obtained from the appendix. Because the sponsor wanted traceability of the factors, only publicly available data was used. Only when no public data could be found, data from private sources was used such as GaBi.

4.1.1 GaBi

The University of Stuttgart developed the software *Ganzheitliche Bilanzierung* (GaBi) which is now distributed by PE International. Elementary flows and processes are calculated from cradle to grave including all emissions occurring during the lifecycle of the product. Various possibilities for the calculation and complex interpretation options are offered by the system. Since GaBi balances according to ISO standards, calculations factors have been extracted from this software. Because the software uses private data it was only used exceptionally.

4.1.2 GEMIS

The software GEMIS was developed by the institute of applied ecology, Freiburg. The public database consists of life cycle data for means of production, but focuses on devices for heat and electricity production. Since the software is public, users can save calculated data for processes or resources. Therefore only validated data by the institute was used for this study.

---

[24] MIN08ME, page 25

4.1.3 GHG Protocol

The Greenhouse Gas Protocol was developed by the WRI and the WBCSD and offers many tools for the calculation of CO2 emissions. The classification of direct and indirect GHG emissions can be obtained from Figure 6: Overview of Scopes and Emissions along the Value Chain.

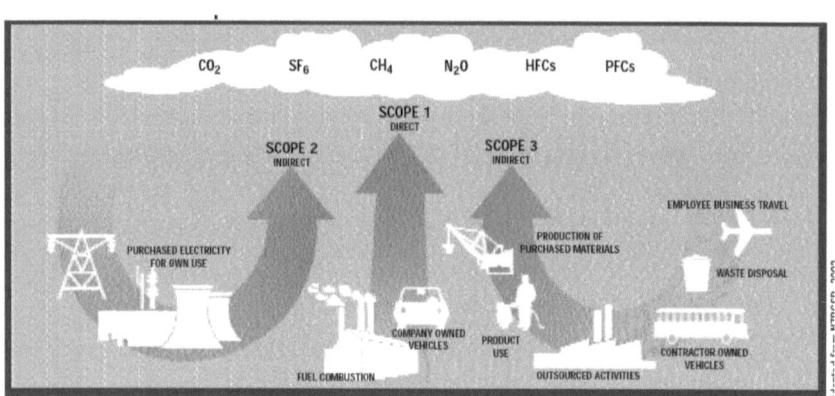

Figure 6: Overview of Scopes and Emissions along the Value Chain[25]

Direct or scope 1 emissions occur from sources that are owned or controlled by the company such as emissions from the combustion of controlled boilers or vehicles. Scope 2 emissions are accounted through the utilization of bought electricity generated at external facilities.

All other indirect emissions are summed up to Scope 3 emissions. These include means of production used by the company but produced at external facilities. Examples are the transport of purchased fuels and the production of purchased materials. These emissions can be reported separately.

The differentiation is introduced because double counting has to be excluded. Double counting can be explained by the following example (see also Figure 7).

An electricity company defined as Generator A reports the generation of 20 t CO2 Equivalents (= 100 MWh electricity) as scope 1, because the emissions occur within the company's border. A utility company C is consuming 5 MWh (= 1t CO2 Eq.) and passing 95 MWh to the end-user. Because the emissions are already reported,

---

[25] WR04CO page 26

company C only reports the utilized energy as scope 2 emissions and the passed 95 MWh as scope 3. The end user consumes the 95 MWh and reports the equivalent of 19t CO2 as scope 2 emissions while the 1 t is reported as scope 3. The cumulated results show no double counting as scope 1 = scope 2 = scope 3 = 20 t CO2 Eq.

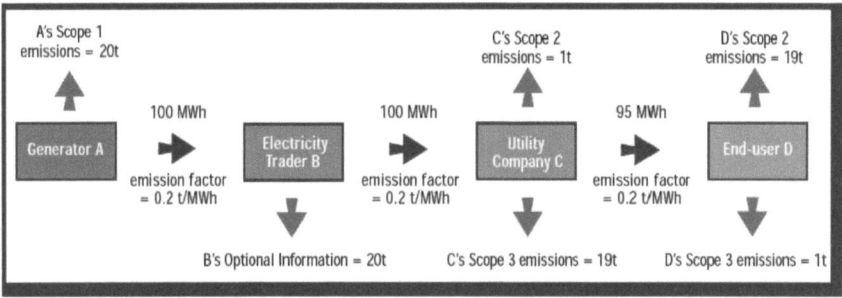

Figure 7: GHG Accounting from the Sale and Purchase of Electricity[26]

Since the GHG Protocol is established and widely accepted, the transportation emissions are calculated with this standard.

4.2   *Emissions of Production Materials*

The means of production are separated according to Figure 5: Defined Flower Production Model. In the following the calculation of these flows is explained.

4.2.1 Emissions of the Production of Package Material

The packaging materials include paper to separate flower bunches, plastics to protect the flowers and a carton box.

Paper:
It was remarkable that paper producers report low emissions per kg paper produced. The values from two providers stated approximately 0,25 kg CO2/kg paper produced. A study by a media association came to the conclusion that this value is only realistic for about 4% of the paper production. Many sources stated emissions between 1 and

---

[26] WR04CO page 29

2 kg CO2 per kg paper. Since LCA software publishes 0,73 g CO2 / kg paper this value was used.[27]

Carton:
The average of GEMIS data and results of a German study by the German environmental agency have been used with 0,5 kg CO2 /kg carton produced.

Plastics:
GaBi and the GEMIS software data resulted in 2,54 kg CO2 emissions per kg plastic used.

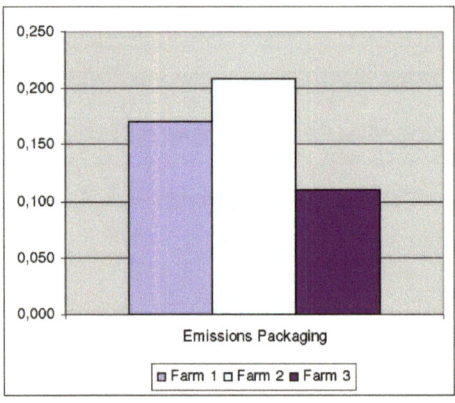

Figure 8: Emissions Packaging[28]

The results show that farm 3 used almost half of the amount of packaging per flower compared to farm 2. Although further investigation has been done with the farm, no errors could be found. Since the emissions of packaging are comparable low, the differences have been neglected. Nils Jungbluth came to the same conclusion in his dissertation.[29]

4.2.2 Emissions of the Production of Chemicals

Chemical production was divided into production of fertilizer and pesticides. Fertilizers accelerate the growth of the flowers while pesticides are used to kill pests and protect the flowers from mushrooms and pest plants.

---

[27] see Figure 38: Emission Factors and Sources for Paper for more details
[28] Illustration by author
[29] JUN00UM, page 49

The main ingredients of fertilizers are nitrate (N), phosphor (P) and potassium (K). Recent studies[30] proof that the production of these ingredients account for the most GHG emissions for fertilizers. Thus, the N-P-K relation for each fertilizer has been asked for, at least 5 fertilizers. The calculation of emissions based on the N-P-K composition lead to the emissions and was related to the total use of fertilizers. Because there is a great variety of fertilizers and producers do not publish detailed emissions which can be related to the final products, emission factors from literature have been used.

Fertilizer with the main ingredient nitrate such as ammonium nitrate, ammonium sulphate or calcium nitrate were calculated with 2,15 kg CO2/kg used. The factor represents a weighted average on investigated LCA data.[31]

Analogue P-Fertilizer was calculated with 0,7 kg CO2/kg and K-Fertilizer with 0,48 kg CO2/kg fertilizer.

There are various methods to account for the emissions of pesticides. But due to the fact that the application of pesticides with different active ingredients varies, exact calculation is complex[32]. Therefore one value has been assigned for the usage of pesticides which was extracted from GEMIS and GaBi.

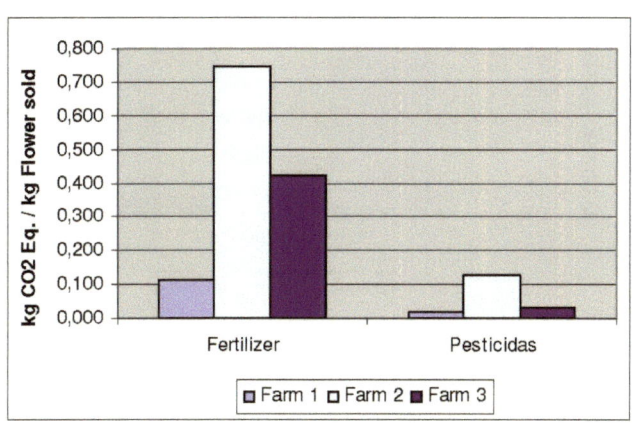

Figure 9: Emissions of Chemicals Application[33]

---

[30] NE04MO, page 5 and WO04RE
[31] see Figure 33: Emission Factors and Sources for Fertilizers for more details
[32] JUN99CA, page 34ff
[33] Illustration by author

The results show that emissions from chemicals differ highly. One reason is that farm 2 and 3 use about 5 times more fertilizer per hectare compared to farm 1. Differences in utilization are also the reason for different emissions of pesticides. Although the climate regions of those farms are different it should be investigated if the application of chemicals could be reduced (cf. Chapter 5).

4.2.3 Energy Consumption on the Farm

Besides electricity also the fuels used for internal transportation on the farms and the operation of generators have been aggregated in Figure 10.
The sources for the two factors are the Oficina Nacional de Promoción del MDL de Ecuador (CORDELIM), which calculated the emissions to produce 1 kWh of electricity with the current energy mix of Ecuador. [34] The result is 0,65386 kg CO2 for 1 kWh electricity. Secondly the GHG protocol has been used for diesel, gasoline and gas emissions.

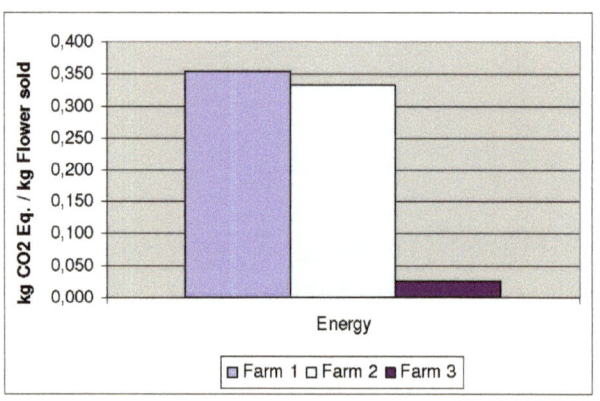

Figure 10: Emissions for Energy Usage on the Farms[35]

Firgure 10 shows that Farm 3 needs significantly less electricity. Since no errors in the data collection could be found this shows that consumption of electricity is a reduction potential for the other farms.

---

[34] COR06EMI, page 4
[35] Illustration by author

4.3 Emissions of Building Construction and Land use Change

The area of flower production consists of greenhouses and office buildings.
Greenhouses are buildings with a light metal construction and surrounding
polyethylene film. Emissions are extracted from Gemis and GaBi.
Office buildings are used for 20 years and calculated with the buildingcarbonneutral
calculator[36]. Office paper was equalized with paper described in 4.2.1.
The IPCC Soil Carbon software[37] was applied for the calculations of change in land
use. Carbon stocks are calculated by the software before the cultivation of flowers
and after. The result was measured in MgC/ha/year. For the transformation in CO2
the following calculation steps have been applied.

1 Mg C ≈ 1 metric ton Carbon (C)

Molar weight of C: $M_C = 12$ g/mol

Molar weight of O: $M_O = 16$ g/mol

Molar weight of CO2: $M_{CO2} = 44$ g/mol

The relation of CO2 and C (44/12) results in 3,67.

Subsequently 1Mg C ≈ 3,67 t CO2

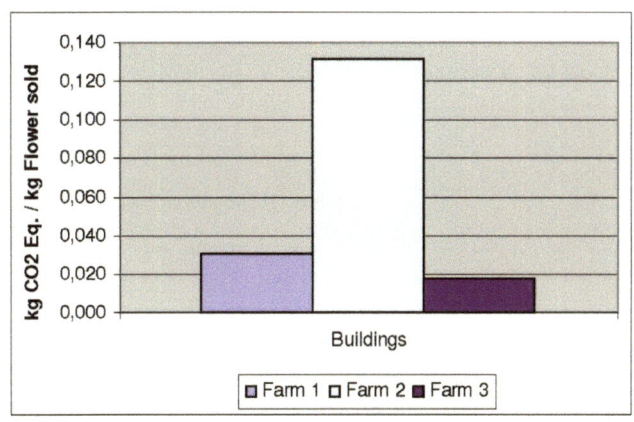

Figure 11: Emissions Buildings[38]

---

[36] BU08CA
[37] IP08SO
[38] Illustration by author

Since fertilizers are applied in a highly manner, the extraction of Carbon from the ground is very low. The office buildings are used over a period of 20 years and therefore the relative contribution to the CO_2 footprint remains on a low level. Farm 2 has more emissions because the consumption of polyethylene for the greenhouses is about 5 times higher in comparison to the other farms.

4.4 Emissions based on Transportation

Mobility has received a strong growth over the past years. Figure 12 shows the rise in personal and freight transportation within the EU from 1985 (Index =100) to 1997. This trend takes place worldwide. The reasons are multilateral. Globalization and more cross-linked companies cause this development. Governments keeping transport costs low in form of e.g. releasing taxes for kerosene in order not to interfere economical growth. The parallelism between transportation and economical growth in form of gross domestic product (GDP) can be obtained from the figure 12.

In the production of flowers, transportation can be grouped into three parts to give further knowledge about possible reduction potential: Personal transportation, transportation of chemicals and flower transportation.

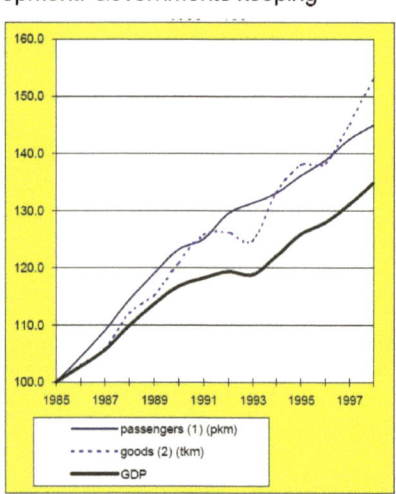

Figure 12: Growth in Transportation within the EU[39]

[39] EU00TRA, page 9

4.4.1 Personal transportation

Farm executives travel to partners in Ecuador and to the final markets in Russia, the US and Europe to increase sales volume. This was calculated in this step just as the transportation from employees to the farms.

The GHG protocol has been used to calculate emissions related to personal travel.

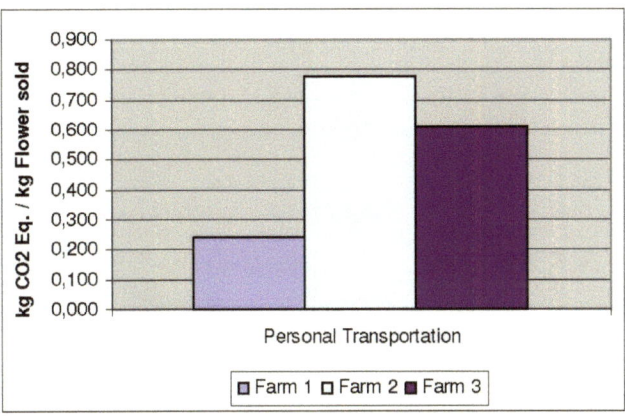

Figure 13: Emissions of Personal Travel[40]

The majority of the employees of farm 1 live close to the employer. Therefore the emissions calculated per flower sold are lower.

---

[40] Illustration by author

4.4.2 Transportation of Materials to the Farm

All the materials needed for the production of the flowers have been calculated separately. These include miniplants being transported from the breeders, office paper, fuels for the use on the farm and chemicals. Chemicals have been produced mostly outside Latin America before they are transported by airplane, ship and truck to the farms. Transportation was calculated with the ratio of 90% ship freight and 10% road freight according to the GHG protocol.

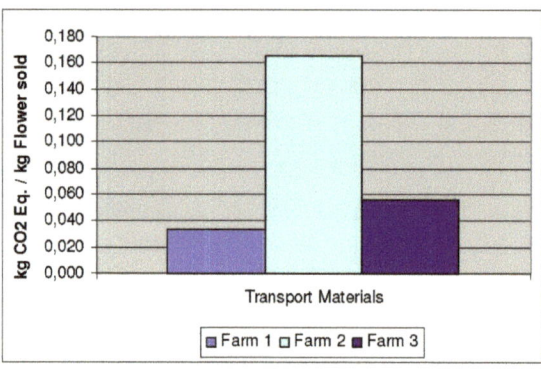

Figure 14: Emissions of the Transportation of Materials to the farm

Farm 2 has higher emissions because the transport of fertilizer and pesticides are the main contributors within materials. Since farm 2 uses the most chemicals, it also has the highest related transportation emissions.

Generally the contribution to the total emissions per kg flower is very low.

4.4.3 Flowers Transportation

Flower transportation consists of the flowers being transported by trucks to the airport in Quito, the air freight and the road transportation to the final vendor.

The GHG Protocol was used with the emission factors for air- and road freight measured in kton (kilometre tonnes).

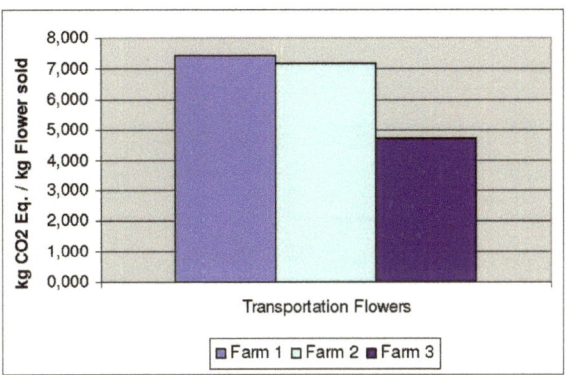

Figure 15: Emissions from the Transportation of Flowers[41]

It can be seen in Figure 15 that the transportation of flowers with about 5 – 7 kg CO_2 per kg flower has a high overall impact. The differences are according to differences in the weight of one flower. While farm 1 and 2 calculate with 70 and 63 gram per flower, farm 3 calculates with 88 gram. Therefore the productivity of farm 3 is up to 70% higher that the other two farms. This leads to relatively less emissions per flower.

---

[41] Illustration by author

4.5 *Waste*

The package used for transportation finally ends in recycling processes or burning stations in the country where the flowers have been sold. Since recycling cannot be assumed for many countries, the factor of GEMIS for consumer waste has been applied. While transportation material (paper, plastics and carton) was considered, the weight of the flowers was neglected. Flowers have been assumed as CO_2 neutral because they absorb CO_2 during the growth period.

Figure 16: Emissions based on the Waste of Packaging[42]

The factor waste has no high impact on CO_2 emissions. The differences are justifiable because they are due to different assumption on the weight of one flower (see Chapter 4.4.3).

---

[42] Illustration by author

4.6 *Results*

The different emissions are summed up and summarized in Figure 17. The comparison of the different factors shows that transportation of flowers to the final market by plane contributes with 70 -85% to the total emissions. Personal transportation, usage of fertilizer and energy utilization are the following contributors. The other in the calculation defined factors has minor importance. Therefore the assumptions made in chapter 2.1 about significant factors are reconfirmed.

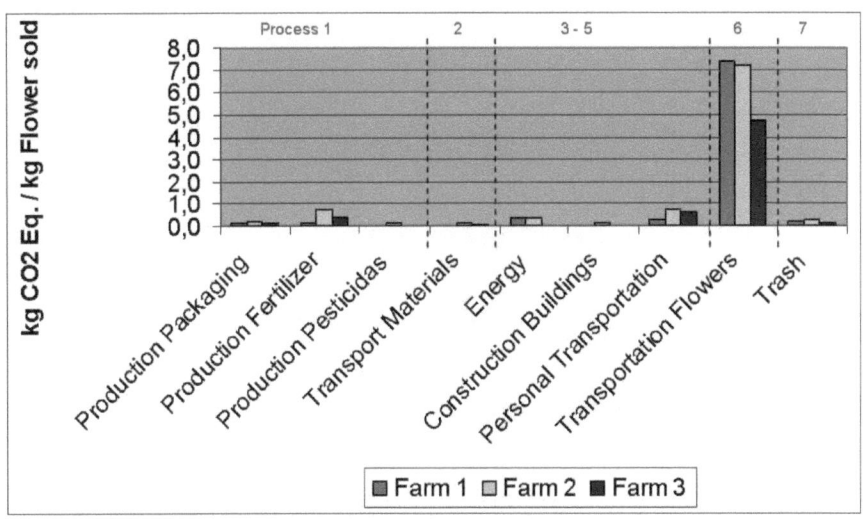

Figure 17: Overview Emissions Flower Production[43]

By looking in detail into the results it can be concluded that there is a high variation in the different processes. Varieties in the utilization of chemicals can be explained by the different climate zones and the different soils. The 60% deviation of farm 3 in process 6 has its reason in the different weight per flower assumed. While the other farms calculate with an average of 63 and 70 grams, farm 3 calculates with 88 grams.

---

[43] Illustration by author

5 Recommendation for Further Steps

The analysis of the CO2 emissions is the beginning of the project FLP CO2 neutral. In order to receive this status the calculations have to be certified and compensated. Parallel it should be investigated how the emissions can be reduced by the farm organisations.

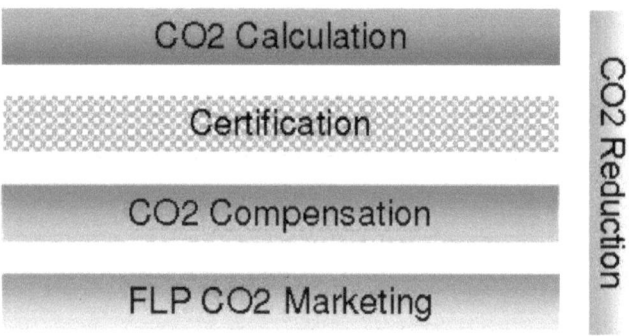

Figure 18: Next Steps towards CO2 neutrality[44]

5.1 *Reduction of Emissions*

The emissions based on aviation are hard to reduce because other forms of transportation (e.g. by ship) need more time and the quality of the roses cannot be assured during the longer time of transportation. However aviation is the main block of emissions and thus is should be investigated if reductions are possible.

Personal transportation can be reduced by changing the fuel system of the farm-owned vehicles. Vegetable oil causes lower emissions than diesel. In some farms diesel generators supply the farms with electricity if there is a blackout. When these generators are renewed the fuel supply should be changed if possible.

The results show different utilization in the application of chemicals and the utilization of energy. Within the FLP CO2 neutral program it should be investigated, how farms can reduce their energy intensity by learning from each other.

Generally the criteria CO2 emissions should be part of the procurement criteria. This means that local produced products should be bought before European products which include long transports.

---

[44] Illustration by author

Many studies are available on efficiency in office buildings[45]. The operation of renewable energies should be investigated since this will reduce the emissions based on electricity generation.

While reduction potentials have to be realized, the current calculation should be certified and preceded.

5.2 Certification

There are various third party organisations certifying GHG calculations independently. Although a general standard is still missing, the certifier checks the traceability of the calculations from the current state of the art. This certification is the basis for compensation of the GHG·emissions. The German institute for energy, ecology and economy (DFGE) for example assigns calculations the label "validated CO2 audit investigation".[46] This is the basis for compensating the emissions, also called offsetting.

5.3 CO2 Compensation - Offsetting

The certified emissions are the basis for carbon offsetting. Carbon offsetting is a financial instrument representing a reduction in GHG emissions. There are two primary markets for carbon offsets. The larger compliance market and the smaller voluntary market. In both markets companies, individuals and governments purchase carbon offsets to mitigate their own GHG emissions.

Alternatively new reforestation projects could be started which might receive CO2 certificates in the future. Since this way is more time consuming and complicated, it is recommended to buy CO2 certificates on the market. If an independent project is intended this could be started and the purchase reduced as certificates are generated from that project.

---

[45] AS04SM is one example
[46] DF08ACC

5.4   CO2 Neutral Marketing

After the emissions are compensated a label should be used to introduce the new product into the market. The label guarantees, that the CO2 neutrality is certified by a third party organisation. This is very important because currently many companies apply "green washing".
This marketing trend means that products are advertised as being very ecological although no environmental development has taken place. The reason why one of these products is very ecological is made up be the marketing department of the companies. It is not very

Figure 19: CO2 Neutral Marketing

transparent why the product is ecological and what measurement has been used. Therefore comparison is not possible and the customers are confused. It is hard for them to distinguish between green products and "green washed products".
Using a well known label helps the promotion of CO2 neutral flowers because the label implies objective judgement. Most of the labels have regulations that have to be met by products in order to receive the label. These standards are public and can be judged by clients.
Labels are a form of quality assurance with well established relations to the customer. The flower farm can profit from these relations.
One of the established labels on the CO2 market is the "CO2 neutral" Label by the German 3C climate change consulting GmbH. Another example is the British Carbon Trust Label which works together with companies to establish the standard informing about the emissions for 100g of generic product.

6 Discussion and further Research

Discussion

Agricultural systems are more difficult to calculate than industrial products. Therefore it has been put a lot of effort in the complete collection of production data. The data from the last FLP audits in 2008 was used to compare the correctness of the received data from the farms. Surprisingly there have been differences (e.g. size of the farm, utilization of pesticides and electricity).

Variations in the application of fertilizers and pesticides can be accepted, because the production of the flower farms takes place on various altitudes with different soil, humidity and climate. Because the effects are low compared to aviation emissions, the differences could not be seen in the total results. But it should be clarified with the certifier if the different assumptions for the weight of one flower are acceptable or if they are normalized to a certain weight. This would reduce disparity.

During the studies scepticism about the stimulation of flower distribution through CO_2 compensation came up. Only higher costs have been contemplated. But these costs should be seen on a broader scale. Firstly more obligations will be introduced by governments to reach the Kyoto goals. Secondly this project has a role model character which could include flower farms in other regions. According to a CO_2 calculation by myclimate[47], examined flowers produced in the Netherlands have four times higher CO_2 emissions per kg flower than those produced in Ecuador. This is a comparative advantage according to David Ricardo: "*Under a system of perfectly free commerce, each country naturally devotes its capital and labour to such employments as are most beneficial to each. This pursuit of individual advantage is admirably connected with the universal good of the whole.*"[48] This cost advantage currently is not realized. Thirdly consumers are more sensible towards the GHG emissions and about 50% are willing to pay more for CO_2 neutrality.[49]

The research on emission factors showed great differences in different sources. LCA or CO_2 studies often only publish the results. This makes it difficult to retrace the calculation steps and to compare the data. Even if the calculations are public, the

---

[47] MY06UM, page 12
[48] RI21ON, Chapter 7.11
[49] OP07ST

issuer uses internal and aggregated factors and the problem consists. Therefore a general basis for CO2 calculations is strongly needed. The scientists working on the PAS are estimating that a fundamental database will be available in 2010.

Further Research

While the current calculations are brought through the process of certification, further investigation on the reduction of GHG relevant processes and materials should be started as well as investigation about the consequences of chemical utilization.
The investigation on the reduction of chemicals utilization is vital and studies in Germany have been made. The application of pesticides was topic of a study recently published by the German Julius Kühn Institute.[50] It dealt with the introduction of beneficial organisms to protect flowers instead of pesticides. The study found out that the costs in the first two years of the introduction of useful animals were higher. But from the third year the costs are the same as with usual pesticides.
In Ecuador the first biological rose farm proofs that it is possible to produce even without chemicals. The farm also had higher costs during the transition period. These costs have to be invested or subsidized by the government.
A program could be introduced offering flower farms transition credits during the period of higher costs. When the production is at the same level as before savings in form of fewer costs for chemicals can be used for redeeming the loan.

Further a detailed LCA would give answers to the questions as how much contaminative substances of the pesticide enter the ground water and if there is GHG-relevant evaporation on the flowers that exit the greenhouses.

---

[50] RICO6NU

Appendix

Table of Authorities

Internet sources

BS08RE   http://www.bsi-global.com/en/Standards-and-Publications/How-
we-can-help-you/Professional-Standards-Service/PAS-
2050/Related-Initiatives/, visited 13.10.2008

BU08CA   http://buildcarbonneutral.org/, visited 10.10.2008

COR06EM   http://cordelim.net/imagesFTP/108125.Emission
Factor   Ecuador 2004   2006   Without CDM.pdf, visited
22.10.08

DF08ACC   http://www.dfg-energie.de/index.php?id=43, visited 30.10.2008

HA07DO   http://www.handelszeitung.at/ireds-40981.html, visited
17.10.2008

HUB08CMP   Huber, Frank, Online Enquiry, Center of Market-Oriented Product
and Production Management (CMPP), http://www.innovations-
report.de/html/berichte/studien/bericht-107466.html, visited
01.10.2008

IP08SO   http://www.ipcc-nggip.iges.or.jp/public/gpglulucf/annex4a1.html,
visited 01.10.2008

OP07ST   http://www.openpr.de/news/175763/Starkes-Interesse-der-
Verbraucher-an-CO2-neutralen-Produkten-Ueber-50-wuerden-
einen-hoeheren-Preis-zahlen.html, visited 30.11.2008

WI08GR   http://en.wikipedia.org/wiki/Greenhouse_gas, visited 23.09.2008

WI08LI   http://en.wikipedia.org/wiki/Life_cycle_assessment, visited
09.10.2008

Literary Sources

AS04SM   American Society of Heating, Refrigerating,
          and Air-Conditioning Engineers (ASHRAE): *Advanced Energy
          Design Guide for Small Office Buildings*, 2004

DE04REW   Enviros Consulting Ltd and University of Birmingham:
          *Review of Environmental and Health Effects of Waste
          Management: Municipal Solid Waste and Similar Wastes*,
          London 2004, page 42

EU00TRA   European Comission, Directorate-General for Energy and
          Transport: *EU Transport in Figures, Statistical Pocket Book*,
          January 2000

FL07GU   Flower Label Program: *Guidelines for the socially and
          environmentally responsible production of cut flowers, ferns,
          plants and foliage*, Version 4, Cologne, May 2007

IP07WG3   Intergovernmental Panel on Climate Change:
          Fourth Assessment Report, Working Group III, Chapter 8
          Agriculture 2007

IP07WG4   Intergovernmental Panel on Climate Change:
          Fourth Assessment Report, Working Group III, Summary for
          Policymakers, 2007

ISO07   International Organisation for Standardisation 14040:
          *Environmental management - Life cycle assessment - Principles
          and framework*, 1997

ISO6EN   International Organisation for Standardisation 14044:
          *Environmental Management Life Cycle Assessment
          Requirements and Guidelines*, 2006

JÖ00LC   Jönbrink, A., Wolf-Wats, C., Erixon, M., Olsson, P., Wallén, E.: *LCA Software Survey*, Stockholm 2000

JUN99CA   Jungbluth, Niels: *Case Studies, Research Groups and Results of LCA's for Food Products, Arbeitsgruppen im Arbeitsfeld Ernährung und Umwelt - Methoden der ökologischen Bilanzierung - Stand der Forschung – Folgerungen*, Zürich 1999, page 34-48

JUN00UM   Jungbluth, Niels: *Umweltfolgen des Nahrungsmittelkonsums: Beurteilung von Produktmerkmalen auf Grundlage einer Modularen Ökobilanz*, 2000

LE97DE   Lenggenhager Irene: *Der Großhandel mit Schnittblumen: Eine ökologische Analyse am Beispiel der Rosen für die Schweiz*, Diplomarbeit Lehrstuhl für Stoffhaushalt und Entsorgungstechnik und EAWAG, Zurich 1997

MIN08ME   Minx, J., Wiedmann, T., Barrett, J. and Suh, S., 2007: *Methods review to support the PAS process for the calculation of the greenhouse gas emissions embodied in good and services*, DEFRA, London, UK, page 25

MY06UM   myclimate: *Umweltaspekte im Blumenhandel Studie zur Klimaverträglichkeit der Schnittblumenproduktion*, Zurich, May 2006

NE04MO   Nemecek, T. and Erzinger, S.: *Modelling Representative Life Cycle Inventories for Swiss Arable Crops*, Agroscope FAL Reckenholz, Swiss Federal Research Station for Agroecology and Agriculture, Zurich, September 2004, page 5

PRA99PO   Prather, M., R. Sausen, A.S. Grossman, J.M. Haywood, D. Rind and B.H. Subbaraya: *Potential climate change from aviation*. In

J.E. Penner, D.H. Lister, D.J. Griggs, D.J. Dokken and M. McFarland (eds.): *Aviation and the Global Atmosphere*. A Special Report of IPCC Working Groups I and III., 1999, Cambridge University Press, Cambridge, UK, 185-215

RIC06NU   Richter, Ellen and others: *Forschung und Entwicklung-Verbundvorhaben "Nützlinge"* published at the Biologische Bundesanstalt für Land- und Forstwirtschaft Institut für Pflanzenschutz im Gartenbau, Braunschweig 2006

RI21ON   Ricardo, David: *On the Principles of Political Economy and Taxation*, Chapter 7, 1821

SAU00AV   Sausen, Robert and others: *Aviation Radiative Forcing in 2000*: An Update on IPCC (1999) in Meteorologische Zeitschrift 2005

SC08ROL   Schulz, Dietrich: *Die Rolle der Landwirtschaft beim Klimawandel – Täter, Opfer, Wohltäter*, local land & soil news no.24/25 I/08

TH00TH   Thomas, C., Tennant, T. and Rolls, J.: *The GHG Indicator: UNEP Guidelines for Calculating Greenhouse Gas Emissions for Businesses and Non-Commercial Organisations*, published by UNEP, 2000

WO04RE   Wood, S. and Cowie, A.: *A Review of Greenhouse Gas Emission Factors for Fertiliser Production*, Research and Development Division, State Forests of New South Wales. Cooperative Research Centre for Greenhouse Accounting For IEA Bioenergy Task 38, 2004

WR04CO   World Resources Institute and World Business Council for Sustainable Development: *A Corporate Accounting and Reporting Standard*, March 2004

General Conversion Factors for Energy

To:	TJ	Gcal	Mtoe	MBtu	GWh
From:	*multiply by:*				
TJ	1	238.8	2.388×10^{-5}	947.8	0.2778
Gcal	4.1868×10^{-3}	1	10-7	3.968	1.163×10^{-3}
Mtoe	4.1868×10^{4}	10^{7}	1	3.968×10^{7}	11630
MBtu	1.0551×10^{-3}	0.252	2.52×10^{-8}	1	2.931×10^{-4}
GWh	3.6	860	8.6×10^{-5}	3412	1

Conversion Factors for Mass

To:	kg	t	lt	st	lb
From:	*multiply by:*				
kilogram (kg)	1	0.001	9.84×10^{-4}	1.102×10^{-3}	2.2046
tonne (t)	1000	1	0.984	1.1023	2204.6
long ton (lt)	1016	1.016	1	1.120	2240.0
short ton (st)	907.2	0.9072	0.893	1	2000.0
pound (lb)	0.454	4.54×10^{-4}	4.46×10^{-4}	5.0×10^{-4}	1

Conversion Factors for Volume

To:	gal U.S.	gal U.K	bbl	ft³	l	m³
From:	*multiply by:*					
U.S. Gallon (gal)	1	0.8327	0.02381	0.1337	3.785	0.0038
U.K. Gallon (gal)	1.201	1	0.02859	0.1605	4.546	0.0045
Barrel (bbl)	42.0	34.97	1	5.615	159.0	0.159
Cubic foot (ft³)	7.48	6.229	0.1781	1	28.3	0.0283
Litre (l)	0.2642	0.220	0.0063	0.0353	1	0.001
Cubic metre (m³)	264.2	220.0	6.289	35.3147	1000.0	1

Figure 20: Conversion Tables

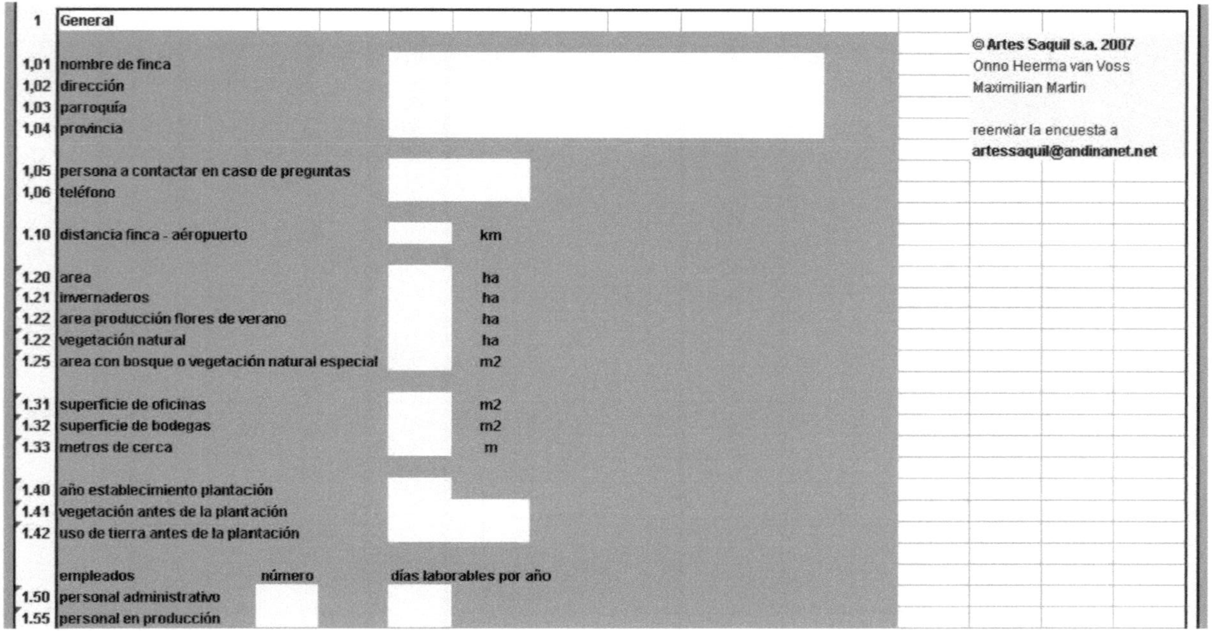

1	General		
1.01	nombre de finca		
1.02	dirección		
1.03	parroquia		
1.04	provincia		
1.05	persona a contactar en caso de preguntas		
1.06	teléfono		
1.10	distancia finca - aeropuerto	km	
1.20	area	ha	
1.21	invernaderos	ha	
1.22	area producción flores de verano	ha	
1.22	vegetación natural	ha	
1.25	area con bosque o vegetación natural especial	m2	
1.31	superficie de oficinas	m2	
1.32	superficie de bodegas	m2	
1.33	metros de cerca	m	
1.40	año establecimiento plantación		
1.41	vegetación antes de la plantación		
1.42	uso de tierra antes de la plantación		
1.50	personal administrativo	número	
1.55	personal en producción		
1.55	empleados	días laborables por año	

© Artes Saquil s.a. 2007
Onno Heerma van Voss
Maximilian Martin
reenviar la encuesta a
artessaquil@andinanet.net

Figure 21: Data Enquiry – General Data[51]

51 Illustration by author

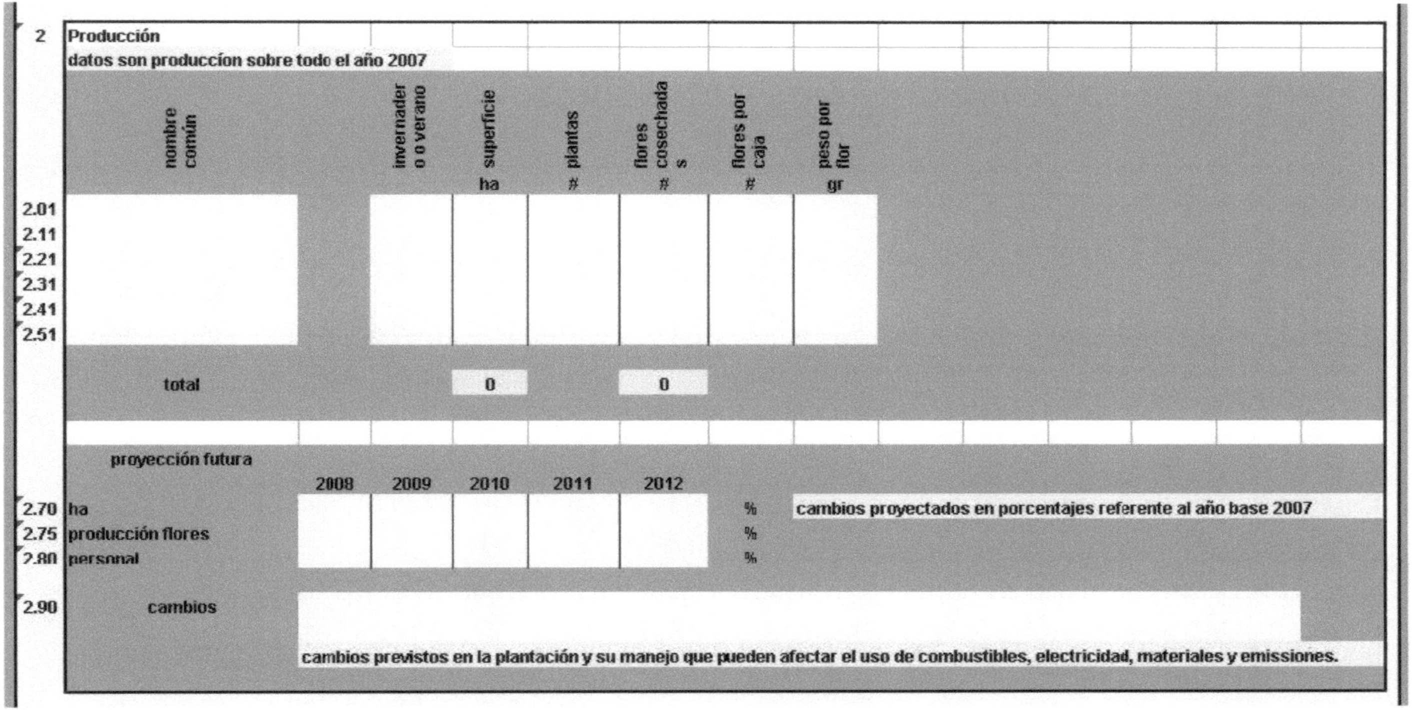

Figure 22: Data Enquiry – Flower Production[52]

[52] Illustration by author

3	Combustibles											
Se trata del uso de combustibles por cuenta de la empresa. No por empresas terceras												
Al mínimo se necesita saber el uso total del combustible por año.												
Datos de uso por actividad (llevar insumos, transporte interno, transporte al aeropuerto) son adicionales.												
		total	unidad	unidad	materiales	interno	luz	aeropuerto	viajes	empleados	unidad	
3.10 Gasolina			galon	USD								
3.20 Diesel			galon	USD								
3.30 otro			galon	USD								
3.40 otro			galon	USD								
3.60 Gaz		tanques	USD	doméstico/industrial	tipo tanque			plantación	oficina	cocina	unidad	

Puede llenar en cantidades absolutas (galones o USD) o en porcentajes

Figure 23: Data Enquiry – Fuels [53]

[53] Illustration by author

4 Transporte

Transporte de personal — se refiere a transporte diario de la casa al trabajo y viceversa

	total	administrat	producción	distancia promedia
4.00 pie o bicleta				km
4.05 moto				km
4.10 carro proprio				km
4.15 buseta de la finca				km
4.20 bus de la finca				km
4.25 buseta de tercera				km
4.30 bus de tercera				km
total	0	0	0	
	%	%	%	
	%	%	%	
	%	%	%	
	debe ser 100 %			

Transporte de insumos

transporte propia / transporte contratado

se refiere al transporte para traer materiales a la plantación

	viajes	distancia promedia	viajes	distancia promedia
4.40 miniplantas		km		km
4.45 insumos de oficina		km		km
4.50 combustibles		km		km
4.55 fertilizantes pesticidas		km		km
4.60 embalaje		km		km
4.65 otros		km		km
total	0	km		km

en caso que no se sabe o puede especificar por tipo de material
se puede poner el total en cualquier de las opciones
la distincción entre transporte propria o de tercera sí es importante

Figure 24: Data Enquiry – Transportation 1[54]

[54] Illustration by author

Transporte al aeropuerto

se refiere al transporte de las flores al aeropuerto

4.75	transporte contratado	
4.70	camión propria	
total	0	

viajes	
distancia promedia	km
cajas por camión	km
tipo camión	

Transporte aéreo

se refiere al transporte aéreo de las flores

destinos	nombre	distancia	vuelos	cajas por vuelo	distancia aeropuerto - mercado
4.100	1	km			km
4.105	2	km			km
4.110	3	km			km
4.115	4	km			km
4.120	5	km			km
4.125	6	km			km
4.130	7	km			km
4.135	8	km			km
4.140	9	km			km
4.145	10	km			km
total	0	km			km

Figure 25: Data Enquiry - Transportation 2[55]

55 Illustration by author

X

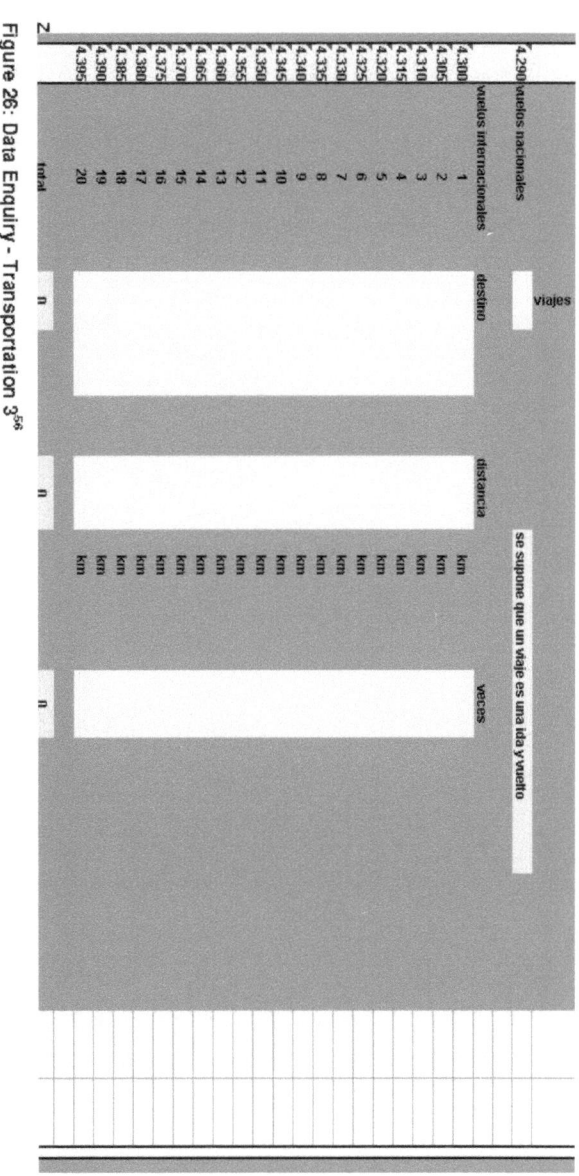

Figure 26: Data Enquiry - Transportation 3[56]

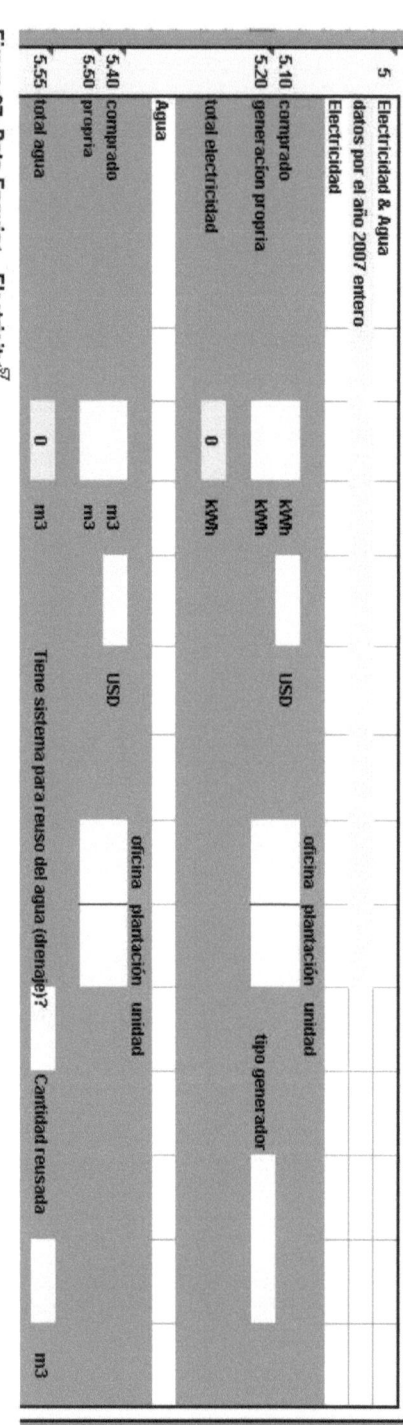

5	**Electricidad & Agua** datos por el año 2007 entero					
	Electricidad					
5.10	comprado	kWh	USD	oficina	plantación	unidad
5.20	generación propria	kWh				tipo generador
	total electricidad	0 kWh				
	Agua					
5.40	comprado	m3	USD			
5.50	propria	m3		oficina	plantación	unidad
5.55	total agua	0 m3	Tiene sistema para reuso del agua (drenaje)?		Cantidad reusada	m3

Figure 27: Data Enquiry – Electricity[57]

57 Illustration by author

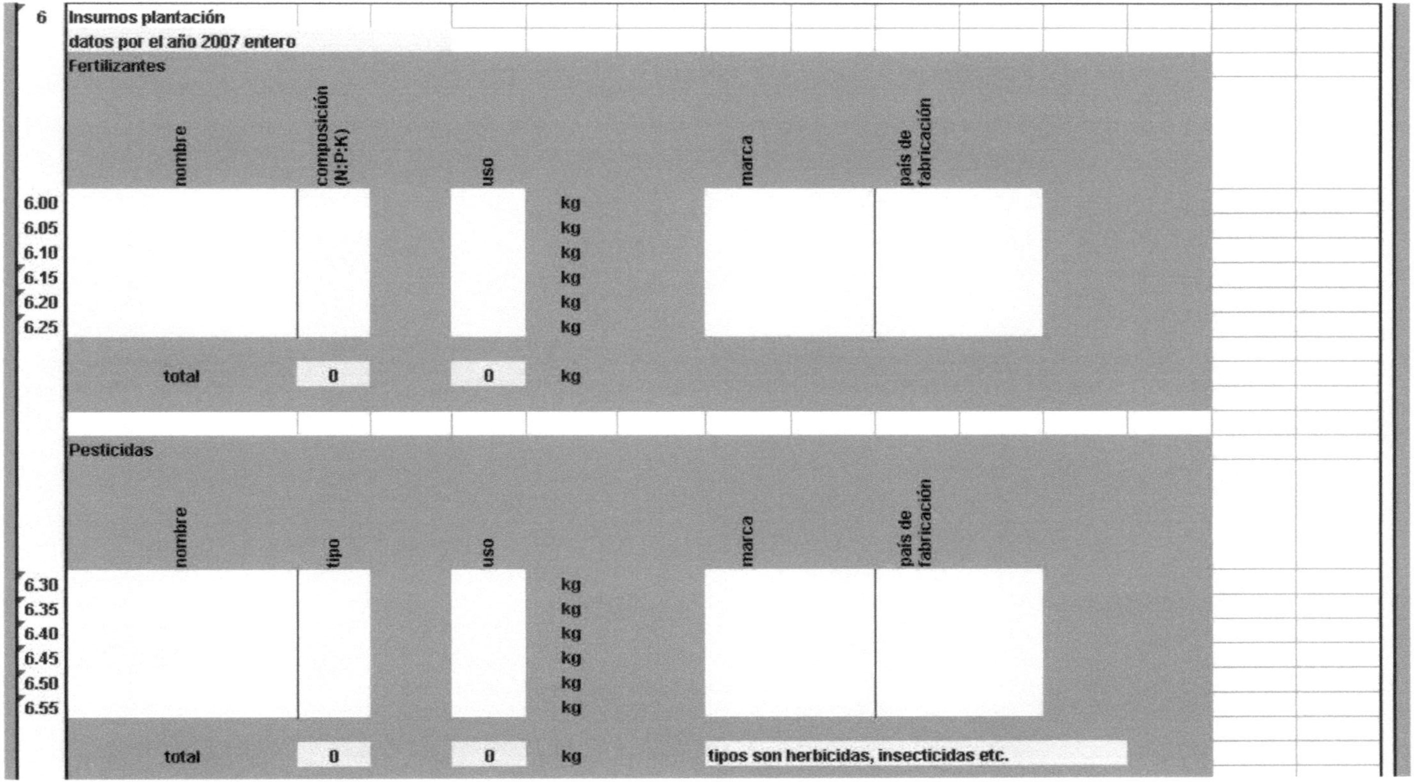

6	Insumos plantación datos por el año 2007 entero						
	Fertilizantes						
6.00		nombre	composición (N:P:K)	uso	kg	marca	país de fabricación
6.05					kg		
6.10					kg		
6.15					kg		
6.20					kg		
6.25					kg		
total		0		0	kg		

	Pesticidas						
6.30		nombre	tipo	uso	kg	marca	país de fabricación
6.35					kg		
6.40					kg		
6.45					kg		
6.50					kg		
6.55					kg		
total		0		0	kg	tipos son herbicidas, insecticidas etc.	

Figure 28: Data Enquiry – Chemicals[88]

[88] Illustration by author

7	Embalaje		se refiere a materiales usado para embalaje de flores (cajas de cartón, paletas etc.)
	Empaques		
7.01	plástico	kg	
7.02	cartón	kg	
7.03	madera	kg	
7.04	otro	kg	
	Insumos invernaderos		se refiere a uso anual de materiales para el mantenimiento de los invernaderos
7.10	plástico para invernaderos	kg	
7.12	aluminio para invernaderos	kg	
7.14	cemento	kg	
7.16	ladrillos	kg	
7.18	madera	kg	
7.20	otro	kg	
7.22	otro	kg	
	Otros insumos		se refiere a uso anual de insumos
7.30	ropa protector	kg	
7.32	papel de oficina	kg	
7.34	otro	kg	
7.36	otro	kg	
	Insumos mechanicos		se refiere a uso anual de insumos
7.40	aceite	galones	
7.42	otro	kg	
7.44	otro	kg	
	Residuos		

			destino	descho	aprobdo	anach'rodh	%	total
7.50	quimicos	kg						0
7.52	vegetales	kg						debe ser 100%

Figure 29: Data Enquiry – Packaging[59]

[59] Illustration by author

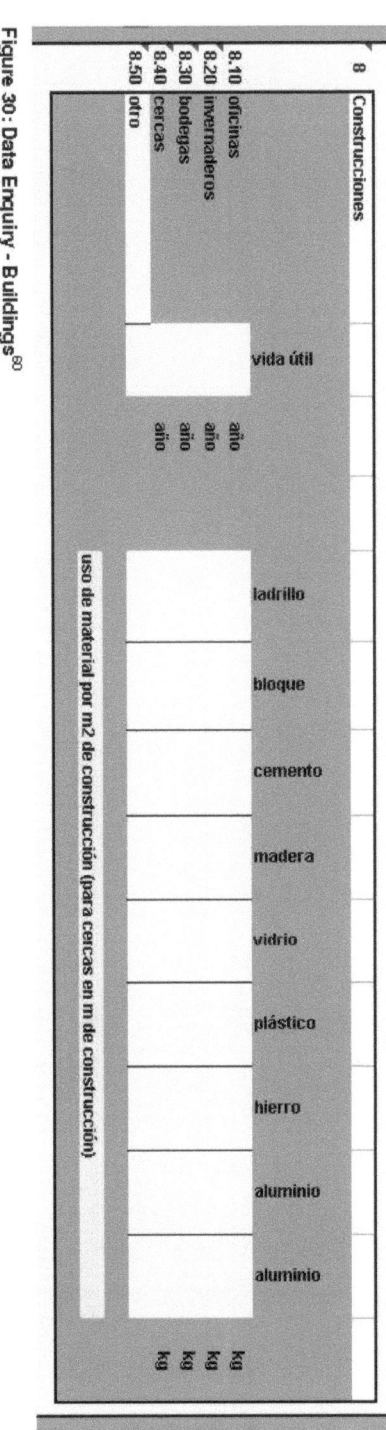

Figure 30: Data Enquiry - Buildings[60]

[60] Illustration by author

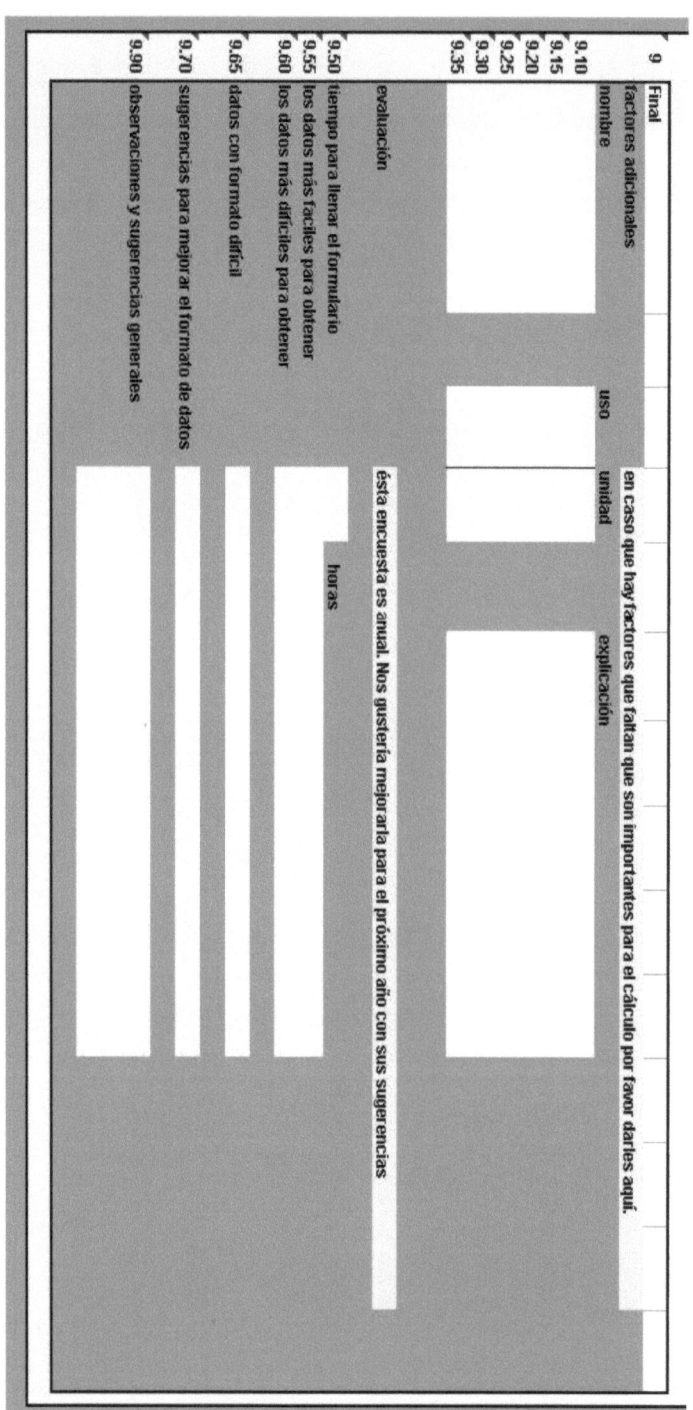

Figure 31: Data Enquiry – Feedback[61]

[61] Illustration by author

Category	Type	Consumption kg GHG/ (kg/kWh/ha) Typ	GHG	Year	Country	Source	Calculation	Argumentation
T1 [4.0 ff]	Diesel [pass. km] Transport of Employees to work	0,1662	CO2	-	World	ghgprotocol_mobile_co2.xls -> emisions based on distance -> bus (diesel)- urban transit	0,1862 kg CO2 / passenger kilometer	Because this factor is minor it was facilitated that all motor transportation to work was made by bus run by diesel
	Gasolina [l] Transporte de Viajes [3.1] Personal to work [4.0 ff]	2,3822	CO2	-	World	ghgprotocol_mobile_co2.xls -> emisions based on fuel -> road transportation -> gasolina	1 l Gasolina = 2,3822 kg CO2 Eq.	
T2	Diesel [l] Uso interno [3.1]	2,75	CO2	-	World	ghgprotocol_mobile_co2.xls -> emisions based on fuel -> road transportation -> diesel (litres)	1 l Diesel = 2,7458 kg CO2 Eq.	
T3	Diesel [l] Transporte de Viajes [3.2] corsumo interno + luz [3.2]		--	--	--	see ghg business travel.xls		
T4	Transport of Personal during work flights [4.29 ff]							
T5 [km]	Transportation of Goods to Finca [4.4] o Flowers to Airport [4.1 (contrato)]	0.43	CO2		World	ghgprotocol_mobile_co2.xls -> emisions based on distance -> diesel light truck 15 mpg 0,430 kg CO2 / kilometer		
T6	Diesel [l] Transporte Flowers Airport [3.2]	2.75	CO2		World	ghgprotocol_mobile_co2.xls -> emisions based on fuel -> road transportation -> diesel (litres)		
T9	Air Transport Flowers	1.58	Co2		World	ghgprotocol_mobile_co2.xls Airfreight	short haul (<452 km)	
T8	Air Transport Flowers	0.30	Co2		World	ghgprotocol_mobile_co2.xls Airfreight	medium haul (452 to 1600 km)	
T7	Air Transport Flowers	0.57	Co2		World	ghgprotocol_mobile_co2.xls Airfreight	long haul (~1600 km)	
T10	Water Freight [t kil]	0.01	CO2		World	ghgprotocol_mobile_co2.xls Marine Shipping (1 t kil = 0,0* kg CO2)		
T11	Road Freight [t kil] [4.1 flowers to market]	0.36	CO2		World	ghgprotocol_mobile_co2.xls Roadfreight (0,072 t kil)	Asumption: 51 pro Camion 51 * 0,072 CO2 à kil = 0,36 kg CO2 / km	
T12	Chemical Freight [t kil]	0,045	CO2	-	World	-	Asumption: The chemicals are shipped to Ecuador, but 10% of the transport is made my trucks.	
T13	Trash final Market [kg]	0,741	CO2	2000	Germany	GEMIS: MVA-Hausmüll	10% *0,01 [T10] + 90% * 0,36 [T11] = 0,045	

Figure 32: Emission Factors and Sources for Transportation[62]

[62] Illustration by author

Abbreviations	Type of Fertilizer	N-P-K	kg CO2 / kg Fertilizer KON98EN	kg CO2 / kg Fertilizante KON98EN	kg CO2 / kg Fertilizante ECO04MO	kg CO2 / kg Fertilizante GExxCH	kg CO2 / kg Fertilizante DA99LI	kg CO2 / kg Fertilizante PA96EN
Data Sources	-	KON98EN	KON98EN	ECO04MO	GExxCH	DA99LI	PA96EN	
AP	Ammonium Phosphate	11-49-0	0,30		0,31	-	2,46	-
AP Nitro	Ammoniated Nitrophosphate acid	8-52-0	0,45		0,40	-	-	-
Urea	Urea	46-0-0	0,61		1,47	-	1,8487	-
AN	Ammonium Nitrate	35-0-0	2,38		2,98	-	-	-
AS	Ammonium Sulphate	21-0-0	0,34		0,74	-	-	-
CN	Calcium Nitrate	16-0-0	1,69		1,36	-	-	-
KN (N)	Potassium Nitrate	14-0-44			2,17	-	-	-
KN (K)	Potassium Nitrate	14-0-44			0,35	-	-	-
KN (total)	Potassium Nitrate	14-0-44	1,97		2,52	-	-	-
Average for N-Fertilizer			**1,11**		**1,40**	**2,48**	**2,15**	**2,178**
MAP (N)	Mono Ammonium Phosphate	11-52-0		-	0,30	0,30	-	-
MAP (P)	Mono Ammonium Phosphate	11-52-0		-	0,78	-	-	-
MAP (total)	Mono Ammonium Phosphate	11-52-0	0,31		1,08	-	0,703	-
DAP 1	Di Ammonium Phosphate	18-46-0	0,46		0,69	-	0,8862	-
TSP	Triple Superphosphate	0-48-0	0,17		0,86	-	0,5201	-
SSP	Single Superphosphate	0-21-0	0,02		0,57	-	0,2209	-
Average for P-Fertilizer			**0,24**		**0,80**	**0,70**	**0,90**	**0,263**
MOP	Potassium Chloride	0-0-60	0,34		0,30	-	-	-
SOP	Potassium Sulphate	0-0-50	0,10		0,65	-	-	-
Average for K-Fertilizer			**0,22**		**0,48**	**0,49**	-	-

Figure 33: Emission Factors and Sources for Fertilizers[63]

Since no information on detailed ingredients of all used fertilizers is available, data from literature is used. The literature used can be obtained from Figure 33:. Since the farms use many different fertilizers with different N-P-K variation, a simplification is made. The

63 Illustration by author

fertilizers are categorized in 3 categories. N-Fertilizer, P-Fertilizer and K-Fertilizer. Each fertilizer has one emission factor (kg CO_2/kg Fertilizer).

The information on the ingredients of every applied fertilizer was very low. Therefore only the fertilizers with information on the N-P-K relation were grouped in one of the three groups. After that we calculated an average of kg CO_2/kg fertilizer (with detailed data) and related this factor to the total use of fertilizers.

We divided N-P-K-Fertilizers into 3 Fertilizers, each of these to cover one main ingredient. For example to calculate one N-P-K fertilizer consisting of 12-10-18 we calculated CN with 16-0-0 to receive the same amount of kg N, SSP with 0-21-0 to calculate the same amount of P and respective for K with MOP. After that the three fertilizers (for example 13 t CN, 9 t SSP and 5 t MOP were calculated with the fixed factors (2,15 for N-Fertilizer, 0,7 for P-Fertilizer and 0,48 for K-Fertilizer).

Only Emissions of Fertilizer production are considered. The emissions during the usage of fertilizers are not included.

Category	Type	Consumption kg GHG/ (kg/kWh/ha) Typ	GHG	Year	Country	Source
	Benomyl Chemicals Pesticid Production	12,546	CO2	2007	Germany	GaBi 4, Software and Database for Life Cycle Engineering, PE INTERNATIONAL GmbH, Stuttgart, April 2007, http://www.gabi-software.com/ - Fungizid Benomyl
	Chemicals Pesticid Production	5,3785	CO2		World	GEMIS: Chem-org\Pflanzenschutzmittel
E 1	Chemicals Pesticid Production [6,59]	8,96225	CO2		World	GEMIS: Chem-org\Pflanzenschutzmittel

Figure 34: Emission Factors and Sources for Pesticides[64]

[64] Illustration by author

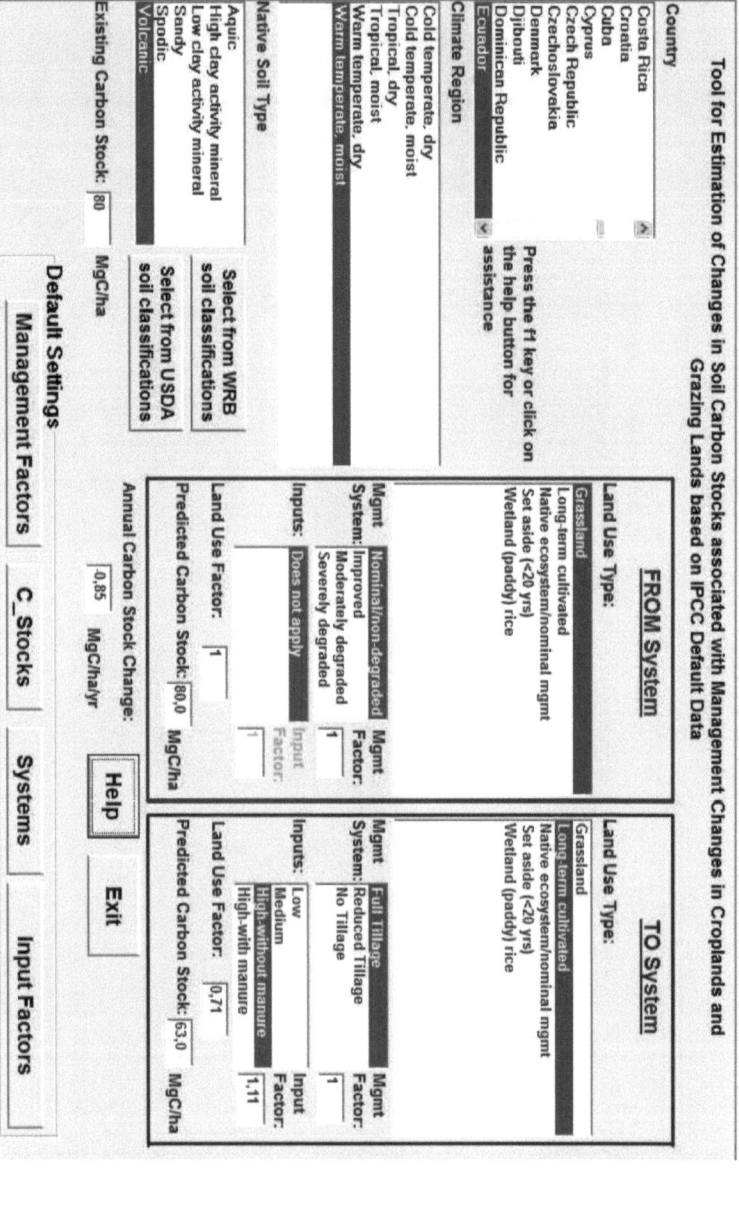

Figure 35: Emission Factor and Source for Change in Land Use [66]

XX

Category	Type	Consumption kg GHG/ (kg/kWh/ha)	Typ	GHG	Year	Country	Source	Calculation
B1	Plastic	1,730		CO2	1995	World	GEMIS: Kunststoffe\Plastik-generisch	Average Consumption per ha invernadero: Finca 1: consumption plastics 5505 kg 17,3 ha Finca 2: consumption plastics 29052 kg 15 ha Finca 3: consumption plastics 8000 kg 35 ha Average: 632,35 kg / ha
B2	Buildings			CO2		USA	http://buildcarbonneutral.org/	All Buildings were calculated with a mixed structural system. The Ecoregion "moderate sierra" was chosen as it fits best the regions of the flower production areas. The calculated CO2 amount is divided by 20 years, as the office buildings are averagely used for 20 years.

Figure 36: Emission Factors and Sources for Buildings [66]

Category	Type	Consumption kg GHG/ (kg/kWh/ha)	GHG	Year	Country	Source
P2	Carton (kg)	0,33	CO2	1995	Germany	GEMIS: Papier-Pappe-D-IOT-95
¦	Average	0,68	CO2	2000	Germany	http://www.probas.umweltbundesamt.de/php/themen.php?&prozessid=%7B0E0B2B9E-9043-11D3-B2C8-0080C8941B49%7D&id=91603599368&step=4&search=&PHPSESSID=8d2e7ea6ca60603564c6642d
¦	Average	0,50				
P2	Plastics	1,73	CO2	1995	World	GEMIS: Kunststoffe\Plastik-generisch
¦	Plastics	3,36				GaBi 4, Software and Database for Life Cycle Engineering, PE INTERNATIONAL GmbH, Stuttgart, April 2007, http://www.gabi-software.com/ Polypropylene film _ extended _ PP _
P5	Average	2,54				
P3	Electricity (kWh)	0,65	CO2	2007	Ecuador	http://cordelim.net/imagesFTP/108125.Emission_Factor_Ecuador_2004_2006_Without_CDM.pdf

Figure 37: Emission Factors and Sources for Means of Production

[66] Illustration by author

XXI

Category	Type	Consumption kg GHG/ (kg/kWh/ha)	GHG	Year	Country	Source
-	Paper	1,20	CO2	2001	Switzerland	http://www.fups.ch/pdf/ratgeber_2001.pdf
-	Paper	1,50	CO2	2003	World	http://www.f-mp.de/content/expertenteams/nachhaltige-medienproduktion/
-	Paper	0,83	CO2	2003	Germany	http://www.robinwood.de/german/floss/2003/hintergrund/oekologie.pdf
-	Paper	0,30	CO2	2006	World	CSR Report UMP (in Papier/CRS Report.pdf)
-	Paper	0,70	CO2	2007	Switzerland	GaBi 4, Software and Database for Life Cycle Engineering, PE INTERNATIONAL GmbH, Stuttgart, April 2007, http://www.gabi-software.com/
-	Paper	0,25	CO2	2007	Sweden	http://www.grycksbopaper.com/Upload/Documents/certificates/Paper%20Profile%20G-Print.pdf
-	Paper	0,24	CO2	2007	Sweden	http://www.grycksbopaper.com/Upload/Documents/certificates/Paper%20Profile%20G-Print%20Smooth.pdf
-	Paper	1,30	CO2	2007	Espana	http://waste.ideal.es/papel.htm
-	Paper	0,24	CO2		World	http://www.smurfitkappa.com.co/NR/rdonlyres/B3E6B9C9-43AD-4909-AE7A-079DB13D6D9A/0/IndicadoresdeSostenibilidad.pdf
P1	Paper Average	0,73	CO2			

Figure 38: Emission Factors and Sources for Paper[67]

---

[67] Illustration by author